Advance praise for

The Social Entrepreneur's Guide to Starting a Creative Reuse Center

"If you're thinking about starting a reuse center there's no reason to reinvent the wheel. Learn best practices and top tips from Kelley and Alyssa, seasoned reuse professionals. This book is a phenomenal resource that will help any reuse company grow and thrive."

- MaryEllen Etienne, Executive Director, Reuse Alliance

The Social Entrepreneur's Guide to Starting a Creative Reuse Center

by
Kelley Carmichael Casey, PsyD
and Alyssa Kail

The Social Entrepreneur's Guide to Starting
Your Own Creative Reuse Center
© Kelley Carmichael Casey and Alyssa Kail, 2012

First published in 2012 by
THE CREATIVE REUSE WORKSHOP
www.creativereuseworkshop.org

ISBN 978-1-300-27538-1 paperback

Book design by Jennifer Alvin
Editors: Aaron Duran, Sanne Stienstra and Stephanie Stoller
First edition: October 2012

Printed on post-consumer waste paper

10 9 8 7 6 5 4 3 2 1

Printed in the United States of America

CONTENTS

Introduction

At SCRAP in Portland, Oregon, where we both are lucky to work, we receive dozens of emails, phone calls, and visits from enthusiastic, spirited individuals who all want to know the same thing: "How do I start a creative reuse center in my town?" They've discovered a website or seen an article about creative reuse. They understand the marriage of creativity and environmental change.

We soon realized that if we were to coach each passionate and motivated caller, we'd have little time to take care of other business. That's when SCRAP began the SCRAP USA project (see Chapter 6 about fiscal sponsorships). And, that's when we realized we needed a how-to for establishing creative reuse centers in other communities.

Like anything, it's easier said than done. There's no satisfactory answer to the "how do I do it" question in a brief meeting or phone call. There's no simple eight-step formula. Starting a creative reuse center is a full-on commitment, takes hard work and good community relations, as well as resilience and a willingness to explain your mission over and over to potential stakeholders. It requires a keen eye for cast-off goodies and doodads that manufacturers dump in the waste stream. And it means writing grants, holding fundraisers, and persuading every friend and every friend's friend to volunteer, give money, and donate materials to the cause.

There are numerous delights along the way when starting a creative reuse center. It is rewarding and often incredibly fun work. Creative reuse centers attract the most interesting people and businesses in the community. You frequently discover new partner organizations and civic champions. You hear a new customer exclaim, "I love this place!" or a child squeal with excitement at finding just the right-sized colorful plastic bottle tops for a robot's eyes. Each day is full of surprises. You never know what donations will come through the door—a jar of vintage buttons in the bottom of a box of random art supplies, or a piece of Chinese silk brocade, or a set of black and white photographs of a family's 1954 snowy vacation at Mt. Bachelor.

This guide is meant to be the answer to the social entrepreneur's question, "How do I start a creative reuse center in my town?"

Kelley & Alyssa

1 The Anatomy of a Creative Reuse Center

In this chapter you will learn:

- About a variety of types of creative reuse centers
- The essential elements common to all creative reuse centers
- How to decide what kind of creative reuse center you want to be

What is a Creative Reuse Center?

A creative reuse center is a place full of color, texture, inspiration, and, typically, a little chaos. Donated materials come in. Purchased materials go out. And items that likely would have wound up in a trash or recycling bin are, at best, reused in a sustainable way or, at worst, postponed from entering the waste stream.

A creative reuse center can be an informal repository for leftovers from classroom projects or a 50,000 square foot warehouse bursting with usable materials from manufacturers, businesses, households, and schools. Many creative reuse centers are community-based nonprofits that couple reuse and recovery of materials with education programming.

What are the essential elements of a creative reuse center?
While they may take different forms and approaches to creative reuse, centers have several elements in common:

- They exist to recover and reclaim materials others deem undesirable.

- They make those recovered materials available for a useful purpose.

- The materials creative reuse centers recover are useful for creative projects, generally craft or arts-related. Additionally, they can be used for home décor, teaching aids and other utilitarian purposes.

- They provide a "home" for materials that other reuse and recycling depots reject.

- They change the sustainability conversation by acknowledging that there is value in repurposing materials for strictly aesthetic reasons.

These elements leave room for vast interpretation of what makes up a creative reuse center.

Types of Creative Reuse Centers

Community Resource
The most common type of community-based creative reuse center is a stand-alone, warehouse-type facility that is open to the public. There may be a retail store, workshop or classroom(s) and an area to receive donations. Materials are collected from local businesses, manufacturers, and households and redistributed to members of the community – generally at a low cost. Not unlike a thrift store, some materials are gently used but have outlived the usefulness of the original owner. Businesses that are closing, manufacturers with seconds or cast-offs, and sales reps with outdated samples donate other materials. The materials can be sold or given away. If the center is largely supported by municipal government or a school district, the trade-off for this support may be that materials are made available free of charge to teachers and/or nonprofits. If the center is independent of a larger entity, the materials are sold at a low cost and

the sales help support the center and its programs.

School-Based Resource

There are creative reuse centers that are supported by school districts. Since the district finances all or most of the operation, the donated materials are given away at no cost to teachers. Teachers then have access to creative materials, school supplies, and educational items free of charge. In some cases, teachers sign up for specific days of the year in which they can "shop." In other school district-supported centers, there are a certain number of teacher shopping days per year when all public school teachers can shop for no cost with a valid teacher ID card. Some centers provide teachers with an approved materials checklist or a designated materials area to control the volume of materials per teacher. These centers may be open to the greater community other days of the year and may charge the public for materials.

Member-Based Resource

As the name implies, a creative reuse center can be a members-only service. Members pay an annual fee and generally have access to a limited number of shopping days or limited materials during the life of the membership. Members may have access to workshop space or classes as well.

In-House Project (Museum, University, or School)

Creative reuse centers are popping up in schools, children's museums, and other educational or creative environments. These centers are generally small, collect limited materials, and serve the employees, students, or members of the institution. These creative reuse centers are often not open to the public.

Pop-Up Shop

Especially when just starting out, it can be a challenge to find donated or low-rent space. Pop-up shops (or stores or retail outlets) are temporary spaces that are rented for a day, a week, or a month at a time. This is a handy way to retail reused materials that have been collected and stored in a storage unit. It builds interest, generates immediate revenue, and gets creative materials into the community.

<u>Mobile Unit</u>

Some creative reuse centers operate as mobile units and show up at schools, community events, parades, parks, and parties. It requires a cube van or small truck from which materials can be transported and sold. It generally requires a storage area for collecting and storing materials.

How do I know what kind of creative reuse center I should be?

A creative reuse center typically develops organically. It starts with a vision and a bunch of discarded stuff that is clean and reusable. The shape it takes depends upon the passions of the person leading the project, the materials available, the needs and desires of the local community, and available space.

If you identify as an artist or crafter, the most natural connections will likely occur within the arts community. You come into the project with the perspective that there is intrinsic value in artistic expression with reclaimed materials. Among the likely initial partners will be art schools and departments, crafting collectives, independent artists and crafters, creative industry (advertising agencies, graphic designers), print houses, and clothing designers. You can pursue shared space with an artists' collective. You may find funding from the arts and culture sector.

If you primarily identify as an environmentalist, you will find partnerships and support from the sustainability community. Waste management becomes a valued source of support. You will find networking at Green Drinks (greendrinks.org) and collaborating with other environmental and reuse organizations to generate interest and open doors. Funding will likely come from foundations and corporate sponsors who place a high value on waste reduction efforts and sustainability. Reuse building supply organizations, such as Habitat for Humanity ReStores, may offer initial support. Goodwill, furniture banks, electronic refurbishers, book resellers, and thrift stores may be valuable collaborators.

Both arts/crafts and environmental approaches will include an education component. The visionaries who have strong educational backgrounds will find natural partnerships with schools and service groups. Education about the environment through creative projects is powerful for school-aged kids. As they learn startling statistics about the volume of plastics in the ocean or the destructive nature of methane gas in landfills created by decaying materials, they are experiencing an alternative and creative use for those same materials. Funding for environmental and/or arts education in schools is available in many communities, especially for underserved districts.

We generally accept that if someone is leading the charge for a creative reuse center, they are dedicated to reuse as a lifestyle choice. There are those who feel it is a cutting edge, marketable concept. There may be others who like the idea of being involved in something novel, creative, and community-oriented. These are legitimate and valuable points of view. The only problem with those primary motivations is that they aren't likely to sustain the dedication needed to see a project to completion. For the purpose of this manual, however, we are making the assumption that all involved are fully invested for the sake of reclaiming usable materials and making them available to the community for creative use.

In the Resources section at the end of this book, you will find a list of several creative reuse centers around the U.S. Perusing their websites is a great way to get a flavor for different ways creative reuse centers do what they do.

To determine what kind of creative reuse center suits you best, spend some time with the activity on the following page.

Activity: What Should I Be?

A good way to determine what sort of creative reuse center to pursue is to ask yourself what makes best sense for you given your contacts, interests, skills, and resources.

Be specific about each area and you'll have excellent insight going forward with your project.

Where am I connected in my community?

What kind of activities do I enjoy?

What resources are available to me?

What are my specific skills?

2 The Art and Science of Reuse Recovery

In this chapter you will learn:

- The pros and cons of picking up materials vs. drop-off donations
- How to determine what types of materials you'll take
- How to write your Materials Donation Policy
- How to be strong and stick to your Materials Donation Policy

There truly is both an art and a science to recovering the materials you want and need, and how they can best be reused. Materials will come to your organization in one of two ways: 1) You will spread the word that you are able to accept donations, and people will bring them to you or, 2) You will desire a particular material and search high and low for a source. Look to a manufacturer that has cast-offs and is willing to donate them to you either via pickup by you or drop-off at your location. In both scenarios, you will have to make a decision about the materials; how they fit in with your mission, and how they can help you succeed.

If you have the ability to pick up materials from business, you may want to consider doing so. While you will have to factor in the cost of a vehicle, fuel, insurance, and your time, there are many benefits to having a pickup program. Some such benefits include:

- You make the donation process easier for donors.

- You have more control over the types, volume, and frequency of donated materials. If you're allowed to look around the facilities a bit, you may find materials you can reuse that they didn't even think of...think cardboard tubes, bubble wrap, or end cuts of leather.

- You create a mobile advertisement—if you properly "brand" your vehicle, you can catch the eye of unsuspecting bystanders. Some might even follow you back to your creative reuse center!

- You have opportunities for face-to-face contact with decision-makers. Sometimes when a donation is dropped off, it's by the person that lives closest to your location or that had some extra time, but not the person that you've been in touch with or has the power to make decisions about donating to your organization.

Before even beginning to take in materials, it is best to create a Material Donation Policy that will allow you to communicate to your donors what you can and cannot accept. While you may not have the foggiest idea of the types of materials available to you, you could begin with some really broad guidelines like, "Materials must be clean and donated within the limits of the metro region," or "Wood and metal pieces less than 3'x3' can be accommodated." It's important to not only think about the material itself and its potential for reuse (which we'll elaborate on next), but also the size and quantity you're able to handle at any given time. It's okay to agree to take some, but not all, that a donor has to offer. Having already set guidelines that are posted in the store and on your website will help you to justify your decisions.

So, what types of materials should you take? This is totally up to you and the desires of your audience. Some questions to ask when making decisions on materials are:

- Is this material most appropriate for my organization or better suited elsewhere? For instance, clothing is made of fabric, but is it perhaps better suited for a homeless shelter rather than to be cut up and used for another project?

- How responsibly can this material be disposed of? Of course, reuse is the higher calling in most cases, but there are times when you are buried in paper products and just can't take any more, so if there's nowhere else for it to go, usually it can be recycled.

- How cool is this material? In other words, how likely will my audience respond favorably to this item? Is it colorful? Is it a strange shape? Is it malleable? Are there many of this item?

- What possibilities for reuse does this material have? For instance, a local woodworking shop has two different wood products to donate and you only have space for one type. You choose the bigger pieces of molding that are more ornamental. You decline the random end cuts from 2x4s that are sharp, inconsistent in shape, and very plain.

One of the biggest reasons many of us get into creative reuse is because we see potential in most cast-off materials and we have a tendency to want to divert as much material as possible from the waste stream. There is absolutely no shortage of materials in this world, in your state, or even in your neighborhood. You will have little trouble quickly filling your space once you start looking. Because of this overabundance, we recommend that you not only get very comfortable in saying "yes" to donations, but also in saying "no" to materials that don't suit your needs. If you can become an expert in your region's reuse and recycling organizations, you can educate your donors on the best uses for their cast-off materials.

It's important to never turn away a donation without giving the donor options for reuse and/or responsible disposal. It's also important to remember that you cannot successfully fulfill your mission if you're up to your neck in unsalable materials (a.k.a. trash). To help stick to your Material Donation Policy when someone is insisting that you take the trunk full of block Styrofoam they just brought in, remember that it costs you dearly in precious time, money and resources to dispose of the materials you can't sell.

3 Passion and Motivation: What Floats Your Boat?

In this chapter you will learn:
- About the role passion plays in your success
- About the role of motivation in your success
- How to take inventory of your passions and motivations
- How to determine if you've got the passion for leading the charge

What's passion got to do with it?

We all have strong, compelling feelings. Our temperaments, personalities, experiences, skill sets and preferences inform our passions. For the most part, passion is intuitive, powerful and difficult to quantify. The roots of passion can reach deeply into childhood or a family legacy.

Passion plays an important role in establishing a creative reuse center. Without a compelling drive, it's difficult to stay the course when it gets bumpy. And at times it will get plenty bumpy. But, that's another chapter. Consider how tempting it can be to bail out of a situation when nothing seems to be going right. You'll need an anchor to hang on to during the challenging times. Enthusiasm and passion for the work make up that anchor.

There is no shortage of online inventories to assess your areas of strength and passion. You can find out how to make money pursuing your passion. Or, you can discover the secret to ultimate happiness in a 12-week online course. You can even tune in to a seminar from a charismatic coach who has developed the formula for discovering how to live a passionate life.

The fact is, you know deep down what floats your boat. To help you document your passionate persuasions, there is an activity page at the end of this chapter.

If you are attracted to starting up a creative reuse center in your community, we'll make some assumptions about you. First, you are likely connected to and care about your community. You see a need for a resource and you'd like to lead the charge. You see gaps in community resources and step in to fill them. You are connected to the marriage of art and sustainability. You are either crafty or a hoarder. We'll assume the former.

It is important to get in touch with that element of creative reuse that has the strongest pull for you. For Alyssa, it is that connection between art and sustainability that drives her passion to work at a creative reuse center. With her life-long creative pursuits and environmental education, she likes to blend her two greatest interests into one symbiotic direction. Though, when first entering college, Alyssa was torn between the fun, conceptual, edgy, kooky world of studio arts or art history and the more down-to-earth, practical world of environmental studies. At 18, she felt she had to decide between the two worlds and ne'er the twain shall meet. So, she chose environmental studies and placed arts on the "hobby" shelf. It wasn't until a few years after graduating college that she discovered that the things she had been making and the materials she had been using all this time were called "creative reuse." Not only was there a name for it, but there was a movement, and she wanted to be a part of it.

For Kelley, passion for working in a creative reuse center lies in providing community service from a happy place. That statement may require a little explanation. The three most common areas of passion for someone dedicated to creative reuse are the environment, art/craft, and education. While environmental sustainability is certainly a strong value and lifestyle choice for her, it does not invoke the drive or commitment of a true passion. She loves crafts and crafters, but she isn't hardcore – or even that good at it. And she has a strong interest in education. But not at the level of a burning passion.

In a previous career, Kelley pursued the field of psychology because she believed it was a passionate choice. She wanted to serve the community and make a difference. She was also fascinated with the creativity inherent in human behavior. All those interests added up to the decision to become a psychologist. The second year of the doctoral program, she was pretty sure she had made a mistake. Her passion was community-based – but not so much in hearing story after heart-wrenching human drama. Not a quitter, she stuck with it. It wasn't long after graduation that her original doubts re-emerged. She realized she didn't have the emotional framework for the infinite needs and demands of that difficult work. Community service continued to be an undeniable draw. But she needed to do it in a less stressful environment. Her passion is in serving the community and her loves include the environment, creativity and education.

Motivation

Motivation, fueled by passion, is what will get the work done. While related to emotion, motivation is not a feeling. If we wait to get the feeling to create a business plan, chances are that day will never come. But, if we are driven by the idea of having success in the creation of a project, we can be motivated to get the damn thing done.

Psychologists refer to two kinds of motivation; intrinsic and extrinsic. As the terms imply, one kind of motivation comes from a sense of inner satisfaction at accomplishing a task for reward such as money or recognition. Both types of motivation can work in your favor.

The intrinsic motivation driven by passion may be linked to a sense of accomplishment, pride in leadership, personal obligation or even a fear that if you don't perform this mission, it won't get done. Those are all powerful motivators to do the hard work.

External rewards are valuable as well. If you do a job and do it well, you are more likely to achieve positive feedback from peers, recognition in the community, and a business card that says "Director" under your name. While money is a powerful motivator, it likely won't materialize for a while. If making money is your primary motivator, you're probably not reading this manual.

How do I know if I've got it?

It's worthwhile to figure out early on in the process whether or not you have a lasting connection to the creative reuse mission. Your route to this passion may be as straightforward as Alyssa's or as convoluted as Kelley's.

How do you know if you've got the motivation to lead the charge and stick with it through thick and thin? Check out the activities on the following pages. Working through the exercises can help you zero in on where your passion lies and what factors motivate you. Reflection on your responses will guide your next steps.

On the next page is an exercise to help you get in touch with your passions. After you've completed that, move on to a Motivation Self Quiz to see if it offers additional insight about your level of motivation. Go to the Mind Tools website at www.mindtools.com and search for "self-motivation quiz."

Passion Activity

The next two pages are designed for you to inventory your interests and preferences that point toward your areas of passion. If you're focused and frank in your responses, you will get the most out of the exercise.

Identify five favorite movies or television shows.

Identify five characteristics your closest friends have in common.

Identify five favorite books – including at least two from childhood.

Identify five tasks you strongly dislike.

Identify five favorite memories – including at least two from childhood.

Identify five favorite websites.

My closest friend would describe me as:

Reflecting on your responses, note where you see themes and similarities. Are there surprises? How does this inform your understanding of your area(s) of passion?

4 Nonprofit? For Profit? Hybrid?

In this chapter you will learn:

- About three distinct organizational types

- How to choose the structure that is right for you

- That business decisions are important decisions that must fit your style and priorities

Here's where we get all business-y and start talking about establishing yourself as a legitimate enterprise. After all, a creative reuse center is a legal entity that must be registered with the government and Internal Revenue Service. You've already had an opportunity to identify your passion to start a creative reuse center, so now is the time to tap into it since things are about to get a little dry and left-brained.

Do you have a technique for keeping focused on your dream? Now would be a great chance to use it!

The first step in the process of transitioning from an idea to the real deal is to determine how you want to organize your business. There are several options with very different structures. We'll focus on three types: nonprofit, for-profit, and a combination of the two.

Three Types of Organizational Structures

Nonprofit

A nonprofit is structured under the 501 tax exempt IRS code. While there are several designations under the 501 heading, an organization created for the common good will generally be recognized by the IRS as tax exempt under 501(c)(3). You can apply for your own tax-exempt status or seek a nonprofit sponsor organization. A nonprofit organization is legally governed by a board of directors and must adhere to specific state and federal regulations. A 501(c)(3) is eligible to receive tax-deductible donations, grants, and funding.

A nonprofit structure can be complex. You may wish seek the assistance of an attorney with that specialty to put all the right elements in place. Each state has statutes and administrative rules specific to nonprofit organizations. There are books and online websites that can be very helpful in walking you through the process. For instance, in Oregon, the Secretary of State's website has a "Nonprofit Business Wizard."

Get started by:

- formulating a Mission Statement (see Chapter 9)
- establishing a Board of Directors (see Chapter 8)
- filing Articles of Incorporation with your state
- creating your Bylaws
- creating your organization's budget
- applying for a Federal Employer Identification Number
- getting IRS Form 1023 and Publication 557 to file for 501(c)(3) status—The fee you pay depends upon the budget of your start-up
- checking your state for other specific requirements

For-Profit

Maybe you're not crazy about having a board of directors govern your dream. You may choose to run your creative reuse center as a small for-profit business. You may organize as a sole proprietorship, LLC, or partnership. Each of these business models has its own legal requirements and tax implications. A small for-profit business will have owners or partners. The owners or partners determine the strategic direction for the company.

State websites generally have detailed information about how to set up a for-profit organization in that state. As each state has their own requirements, stick with the steps outlined by the Corporation Division of your Secretary of State's office.

Hybrid

While still a controversial model, a for-profit/nonprofit hybrid can be an option for some organizations. It's a challenge for a sole proprietorship or LLC to attract support from corporations, foundations, and even individuals without the benefit of offering them a tax deduction. It's a challenge for nonprofits to develop a dynamic and competitive business model. An attorney with this specialty can set up a structure where the profits from the business are channeled directly to the nonprofit, mission-driven organization. Microfinance organizations often use this model.

Choosing a model

One of the above organizational structures is likely to appeal to you more than the others. The best fit depends upon your style of doing business and your priorities. There are advantages and disadvantages to each model.

Many of us are happiest when our passions merge with our professional lives. In the nonprofit world, you can have that beautiful marriage. On the flip side, it requires a dedication to accountability and loss of control of the organization that you have helped create.

Others are fiercely independent and don't enjoy reporting to a board of directors who have governance responsibility over the organization. They may have the drive and resources to make it happen without the benefit of tax-deductible donations. It's their baby and they aren't comfortable with others having equal or greater power over business outcomes.

For innovative social entrepreneurs, a hybrid organization may be exactly right. With a strong legal structure in place, there can be latitude for market innovations that are profitable and support a benevolent cause.

These are options to consider while you are developing your business plan. Business plan? Yep. There will be less sexy, but necessary, information in chapters to come. Hang in there, because there's plenty of exciting stuff ahead, too.

A note from the authors
There are plenty of areas in setting up your creative reuse center where you can rely on the advice of friends and others excited about your project. But choosing and setting up your organizational structure is not the place for getting casual counsel. Find an attorney in your community who specializes in small business law to help you identify the best structure for you and get it set up right from the start.

5 A Mother Ship May Be in Order – Fiscal Sponsorship

> **In this chapter you will learn:**
> - How a fiscal sponsorship works
> - How to be an attractive project for a potential sponsor

By now, you've thought about your business structure. If you're leaning toward organizing as a nonprofit entity, there's an option you'll want to consider—fiscal sponsorship.

What is fiscal sponsorship?
According to the National Network of Fiscal Sponsors: "Fiscal sponsorship means a nonprofit organization (the fiscal sponsor) agrees to provide administrative services and oversight to, and assume legal and financial responsibility for, the activities of groups or individuals engaged in work that furthers the fiscal sponsor's mission." In other words, you can leave the humdrum administrative and legal tasks up to the sponsor and focus on establishing your creative reuse center. And focus on raising money. As the sponsor's project, you will have the benefit of using their tax-exempt status. This means that right off the bat, you can offer tax-exempt receipts for donations you receive from fans, friends, family, foundations, and others.

There are several models of fiscal sponsorship, but the most common for your operation is a Model A – Direct Project. In this model, you become a program of the sponsor just like any other program, such as membership, volunteer, or outreach. The sponsor organization brings you "in house" and you belong completely to the sponsor. The sponsor is then an "incubator" or "umbrella" of support and protection for your project. This model is becoming more and more common with arts organizations. Generally, the sponsor organization receives a certain percentage of the project's income in exchange for providing the administrative, financial, and development oversight.

Optimally, you'd find another creative reuse center that offers fiscal sponsorship. What is extra-appealing is that they've already done much of the work. The learning curve isn't quite as steep to climb. They understand the nonprofit guidelines and regulations. They are in cahoots with the reuse community. They have a brand, methods, history, activities, and talented staff to train you and your volunteers to hit the ground running. And they have a commitment to your success and the success of the mission.

How cool is that? Pretty cool.

The fiscal sponsor's board of directors will govern your operation. The sponsor will have expectations of high quality programming, activities, and presentation to the world. They will expect reporting and a structure of accountability.

Being an attractive sponsorship applicant
It will be important to prove to the potential fiscal sponsor that you are a worthy partner in the creative reuse mission. As there is liability involved for them, any potential sponsors will require an application process that will mitigate the risk involved in taking on a project.

To make yourself a truly viable candidate for sponsorship, you'll want to have your homework done well ahead of contacting the prospective organization. Not unlike applying for a grant, you want to present yourself as a solid prospect. There are ways to present to the organization that you will be an asset to them.

Arm yourself with a strong business plan. A forecasted operations budget and fundraising plan will be helpful. An understanding of what it takes to set up a creative reuse center is key. This manual should be helpful in putting together a nice, attractive package.

There is no element of preparation that is more compelling than showing community support for your project. You'll find out more about this in the next chapter.

The Social Entrepreneur's Guide to Starting Your Own Creative Reuse Center

6 Feasibility: Is the Community Glue Gun-Ready?

In this chapter you will learn:
- How to find out what people really think about your idea
- How to find out what people think and dazzle funders with the results

What would be more mortifying than throwing a party and no one comes? All the excellent planning and preparation falls flat if no one is interested in showing up. Generally we have good instincts and imagine that if we find something exciting and compelling, others do too. The problem with that logic is what psychologists call "confirmation bias." People tend to hear or interpret information that supports their own beliefs. If I believe that creative reuse is the greatest thing ever, I may tend toward interpreting ambivalence as a positive response and even subconsciously screen out conflicting information. While creative reuse is the best thing ever, you need to find out if other people in your community agree.

Unless you have sufficient fans and supporters, you're doomed to adopt the status of a "struggling little art supply shop." Who wants that? You want to show off your creative reuse chops. So to get off to a strong start, find out whether you truly have the support of your community to make it happen.

Informally gauging the viability of your idea

One of the best ways to find out how interested people are in your idea is to ask them for money. Seriously. If you can raise a minimum of $1,000 from a large number of people, you likely have enough support to get one foot onto the scene. It's actually a better outcome for you to receive one hundred $10 donations than one big check from Uncle Richie Rich. You ultimately need a contingency of crafty scrappers (or scrappy crafters) to support your mission, donate, and purchase materials at your creative reuse center, and tell all their friends about it.

You could do a traditional feasibility study with surveys, interviews, focus groups, and a three-pound report. But we suggest that it can be as valuable to show up to every networking event, community fair, farmers' market, Green Drinks, roundtable, reuse show, and picnic. Armed with your business cards, flyers (printed on reused paper, of course), interactive activity, and well-rehearsed elevator speech, you'll be able to gauge the popularity of your idea. And, you'll be educating about the mission at the same time. While you're talking about your creative reuse center idea – listen and learn. Watch body language. Note facial expressions. Hear the words without bias. And take notes. Surprise, delight, and disbelief go into the "they love us" column. A shrug, eyes glazed over, or walking away goes into the "they're not really onboard" column. If, when you share your idea, most people have a similar response to a kid getting the big present on Christmas morning, you're on the right track.

Formally gauging the viability of your idea

If you are considering a for-profit venture and will be looking for investors, or you want to hook up with a fiscal sponsor, you may want to invest the time and money in creating a formal feasibility study. Your study will include an analysis of:

- A creative reuse center and how it would work
- How it would benefit the community
- How you will measure success
- An analysis of the market environment
- Successful models
- Competition

- The creative reuse movement
- Your business model
- Marketing and communications strategy
- Service delivery
- Management and personnel
- Rules and regulations of your state
- Risk factors
- A break-even financial analysis
- Final findings and recommendations based on your analysis

Methodology

Primary Research
If you have the resources or bandwidth, you could create a survey and, using Survey Monkey or another free survey service, send out questionnaires to prospective customers. You could follow up with focus groups or individual interviews to gain more insight about the perception of people in your community about the need for a creative reuse center. If you don't have experience doing primary research, you may wish to engage a graduate student, experienced friend, or hire a specialist.

Secondary Research
The Internet possesses all the data you could ever need to support your dream. There is a wealth of information out there ready to be discovered. Here are some facts to gather that can help build a picture of where you fit in the community:

- Volume of waste created in your community each year
- Volume of waste diverted in your community each year
- Government sustainability goals and initiatives
- Reuse players – building supply, furniture banks, thrift stores, reuse material vendors
- Crafty players – local Etsy, craft supply, art studios and programs, arts advocacy

There are loads of other fun facts that you'll gather along the way to help shape your study. For example, you might discover how much of their own money teachers spend on average on art and school supplies for their classrooms.

Quotes and anecdotal experiences certainly liven up a feasibility study. You're bound to get some good responses on surveys or in person when you engage your audience on the topic of creative reuse. Art tends to make people happy – and they can offer colorful tidbits you can sprinkle around your study.

7 Game Plan for Readiness

In this chapter you will learn:
- How to talk about your creative reuse center's concept to newcomers
- How to adjust your language for different audiences

Okay, so you've thought long and hard about it and you've concluded that you're right for creative reuse and creative reuse is right for you. You know that you're passionate about starting a creative reuse center in your town, you have found some supporters and advocates, and you've decided which business model might work best for you. So, you're ready to dive in, right? Well, almost...

Take a few deep breaths and visualize where you are and where you want to go. How are you going to communicate this vision to your community members? You should already have experience with this since you just completed your feasibility study. Think back to when you were talking with potential supporters. Were you able to develop an elevator pitch? That is, a clear and concise but genuine description of what you're working so hard to achieve. Were there certain phrases or words you used that really caught people's attention?

For example, we find that many people are familiar with building material reuse if they aren't familiar with creative reuse. In that case, you could say something like, "So, you know of building material reuse? Well, imagine a place just like that but with arts and crafts materials instead of 2x4s and old windows." If people are having a difficult time imagining what in the world you could make with materials saved from the waste stream, you could give examples, like cork boards made from wine corks or bottle cap jewelry.

In other words, you are going to be talking to a lot of people about this exciting new organization, and you want those words to matter. In many cases, you'll have mere seconds to engage a potential new fan. Think about what might matter to that person in particular and how your organization could best serve them. If they are a "starving artist," mention the low price point of your materials. If they are a parent of school-age children, talk about the workshops or camps you plan to have. If they are a business with cast-off materials, focus on the benefit of a tax write-off (if you're a nonprofit) for donated materials.

So, now you have your vision and your words.

Practice with the exercises on the next page. It will help you formulate your message – a true necessity of readiness.

After that, if you feel ready, then let's start putting the pieces into place. From here on out, you'll learn how to put it all together: How do you choose your advisory board? How do you write a business plan? How do you find the money that you need? How do you find a physical space?

Language Activity

This exercise will help you think about the message you would want various types of people to know about your organization and how they may want to get involved. Based on the following brief descriptions, write what you would tell them about your creative reuse center in seven words or less.

Example: An undergraduate art student at local university
Answer:
Inexpensive art supplies and numerous volunteer opportunities

Inventory manager at local LEED-certified architecture firm

Recent retiree as art curator

Principal at nearby elementary school

Small business owner that hand crafts purses out of reused materials

Elderly woman downsizing to an apartment

8 Building Your Advisory Board

In this chapter you will learn:

- How to be strategic in selecting your advisory board members
- How to achieve a balanced board
- How to avoid being stuck with the wrong fit on your board

When you decide to move forward to open a creative reuse center, one of your best assets will be your group of trusted advisors. An advisory board is a collection of individuals that you choose based on the strengths they bring to your project. They may be friends, professional colleagues, people you admire in your community, or even those you seek out through referrals or on boardnetUSA.

There is a difference between a board of directors and an advisory board. At this point, unless you already have acquired 501(c)(3) status through the IRS, yours will be an advisory board. Unlike a nonprofit board of directors, they do not have governance or legal responsibility for your project. They are assembled to help you achieve your vision and act as your wise guides.

Learn from our mistakes

We have some strong feelings about boards based on lessons learned the hard way. It's tempting to get so caught up in the excitement of doing your project that you tackle everything at once. Ultimately overwhelmed, you feel grateful for the help of anyone with a pulse. We have one word for you. STOP!

Heed this warning: If you don't choose your advisory board carefully, you will surely regret having made a poor choice of primary advisors. Or you will regret having made a poor choice of even one primary advisor. One advisor who doesn't understand the mission or has his/her own agenda can disrupt the advisory board dynamic to create roadblocks in your forward movement.

There are two rules that we have learned the hard way. You are smart and savvy to be reading this and learning from our mistakes.

Rule #1

Understand what you need before you invite advisory board members. This is the group that will be most influential and instrumental in getting your creative reuse center off the ground.

Rule #2

The single most important characteristic to consider when choosing your advisory board is dedication to your mission.

We have had experiences with smart, capable board members who offered valuable expertise to the organization. However, reuse wasn't already integrated into their lifestyles. They wound up working against our strategic goals because they weren't mission-driven. It can be difficult to move forward with a strong, smart person on your board that doesn't get it.

Consider the following:

Each advisory board member should bring a unique skill to the party. For example, you don't need two attorneys on your board.

Create a diversity of talent and perspectives. Let's say your advisory board is made up primarily of a group of friends you met through the quilting guild. Guess what kind of resource your creative reuse center is going to be? The strength and commonality of your group will probably be around needlecraft and fabric. You'll be headed in a specific direction without much awareness of the diversity of ideas, materials, and programming available to you.

You are creating an arts and environmental organization. A creative reuse center is a beautiful marriage of two disciplines that aren't always seen as naturally connected. You will need champions in both sectors to thrive.

Spend time on the following activities and you will create a clearer picture of who can create a dynamic and proactive advisory board. Then you can develop a job description for prospective board members that will help you, and them, understand the expectations of the job. There are good samples of board job descriptions at bridgestar.org.

Your Advisory Board Needs Assessment

Working through this activity will help you hone in on the areas of expertise that smart, dedicated advisory board members can fill.

What tasks need to be accomplished?

Consider legal review, financial projections/budgeting, connecting with donors, connecting with community leaders, volunteer management, nonprofit expertise, and fundraising.

Now place these tasks in priority order.

Which of these tasks can you or one of your partners do?

List the areas of need remaining.

You now have a good idea of the skill sets you need represented on your advisory board.

What kind of advisory board do you need?
This exercise will help you sort out what the character and focus of your advisory board should be.

Rate the following by:

1- High Priority 2- Medium Priority 3-Low Priority 4- Not a Priority

Board Needs	1	2	3	4
A working board that rolls up their shirt sleeves and gets to work				
Advisors who will give me business advice				
A board of community engagers who will represent us in the community				
Members with deep pockets who will make a significant financial commitment				
Members who are supportive of my efforts				
Members who are available ad hoc when I need them				
Close friends who understand me and my priorities				
Professionals who are well-experienced and objective				
A board that will focus on raising money				

9 Creating your Mission Statement

In this chapter you will learn:

- That your mission statement is the keystone to your organization
- That having a clear, concise statement is essential
- It is worth the time, dedication, sweat and tears to create the right mission statement for your creative reuse center

Whether you become a nonprofit or for-profit, your mission statement is the most foundational business planning you will do for your budding creative reuse center. It will encapsulate your purpose and identity. It will justify your *raison d'etre*. It will inform all of your activities and programming. Having a carefully crafted mission statement will have a significant pay-off for the life of your organization. And, at the end of this process, you will know what direction you're going.

It's important that your mission is a clear, concise statement that says who you are, what you do, and for whom you do it. That's it. Simple enough, right? Well, not always. You'll need to build consensus with stakeholders about the mission from the very start. Stakeholders don't always see eye-to-eye. The process of developing the mission statement tends to fuel lively and potentially heated discussions around the organization's priorities, purpose, values, and target audience. We recommend assembling your advisory board members and partners and set aside a rainy day to focus on this important task.

Once you have created your mission statement, you have a mantra for yourself, board members, staff, and volunteers. You have a ready elevator speech. You have a guiding light for program creation. You also have a gauge for evaluating your programs. If an activity doesn't serve the mission statement, you might question why you're doing it. Every organization wants to avoid "mission drift." Staying clear and true to your mission statement is a great way to stay on course.

Below are samples of mission statements for creative reuse centers. Each organization's reflects their values, activities, and purpose.

Our mission is to inspire creativity and environmentally sustainable behavior by providing educational programs and affordable materials to the community.
SCRAP (School and Community Reuse Action Project), Portland OR

Arts & Scraps uses recycled industrial scraps to help people of all ages and abilities think, create and learn.
Arts and Scraps, Detroit MI

To encourage, inspire and promote fun ways to reuse items and materials "too good to throw away" for creative reuse projects.
Long Beach Depot for Creative Reuse, Long Beach CA

SCRAP's mission is to stimulate creativity and environmental awareness in children and adults through promoting the creative reuse of materials that traditionally have been discarded as waste.
SCRAP Scroungers Center for Reusable Art Parts, San Francisco CA

The mission of the East Bay Depot is to divert waste materials from landfills by collecting and redistributing discarded goods as low-cost supplies for art, education, and social services in our Depot Store. The educational mission is to increase the awareness of school children and the general public regarding the green benefits of reusing materials.

East Bay Depot for Creative Reuse, Oakland CA

All of the mission statements above address the business of creative reuse but with their own twists. Make sure your mission statement reflects your core activities and values. You will rely on this statement over and over again. Think of it as your North Star. It guides the way and keeps you on track.

You should use the exercises on the following pages with your stakeholder group during the mission statement development "party." At the end of that dedicated day, we recommend celebrating big time. You will have accomplished one of the most important tasks necessary to get your creative reuse center up and running.

Putting Together Your Mission Statement – Part 1
You've already assembled your stakeholders and set aside a rainy day to focus exclusively on the mission statement. The first step in that process is to consider questions like the following listed here.

Why are you pursuing starting up a creative reuse center? *What do you want for yourself and the community? What excited you about the opportunity and how will you keep that passion alive?*

What part of the community will you be serving? *What can you do for them that is unique and will enrich their lives?*

What image of creative reuse do you want to convey? *How will you create the impression you want with a variety of stakeholders?*

What kind of programming will you provide? *Don't be vague; define what makes your creative reuse center so extraordinary.*

What kinds of materials will you collect and provide to the community? *What factors determine sources and pricing? Consider how these relate to the reasons for your creative reuse center's existence.*

What kind of relationships will you maintain with material sources and donors? *Every creative reuse center is in partnership with its donors – both material and financial.*

How do you differ from your competitors? *People have limited dollars – how can you be sure they spend with you instead of Michael's?*

How will you use technology, capital, processes, products, and services to reach your goals? *A description of your strategy will help keep you focused on the end goal.*

Putting Together Your Mission Statement – Part 2
Reflecting on your responses to the questions in Part 1, are there consistent themes? Identify them and use them to help shape the reasons for your mission.

Putting Together Your Mission Statement – Part 3

Now you're ready to create your mission statement, with the following steps.

Brainstorm

All ideas are game. There are no wrong or silly ideas at this point. Generate ideas by looking at the sample mission statements in this chapter and thinking about or discussing the questions in the previous section.

Experiment

Next, each person should write an individual mission statement. Read the statements out loud and choose the bits you like best.

Articulate the Mission

Use action verbs. Make the language interesting and descriptive. You'll wind up with a memorable and useful mission statement.

Congratulations!

You've just created the most important statement of your creative reuse center's life.

Celebrate!

That was big.

10 Mobile? Brick and Mortar? Online Exchange?

> **In this chapter you will learn:**
> - Three types of venues for creative reuse centers
> - How to determine which venue is right for you

Now that you've created your mission statement, what type of venue will you need to fulfill your mission?

There are three primary venue types we typically see in the world of creative reuse:

Mobile units
Vehicles of all sorts can take the mission and materials to the community

Brick-and-mortar
Most traditionally a creative reuse center will be a physical location such as a warehouse or storefront

Online material exchanges
You can connect materials with organizations or individuals who need those materials through the internet.

Most creative reuse organizations typically utilize some combination of the three. Choosing the right type of venue will help you to stay true to your mission.

For instance, if your mission is to keep materials out of the land-fill by connecting businesses that have cast-off materials with artists needing materials, any one of these venues could serve you just fine, but let's try to narrow it down. You've got to start somewhere!

Another question to ask yourself is who (geographically) is your audience?

Do you live in a city that is both rich in manufacturing/pro-duction and artists? Is there a neighborhood where you're likely to find an affordable (or free!) building that will be acces-sible by both donors and shoppers? If you answered "yes" to both questions, seems like you'd be wise to start with a brick-and-mortar location.

Do you live in a more rural or sprawling area, where it may be difficult for donors or shoppers to come to a central lo-cation? Perhaps you should choose a mobile model, where you can pick up and deliver materials in a truck, van, school bus, horse and buggy, or any other mode of transportation you can fathom. With mobile unit(s), it's likely that you'll still need some sort of storage building, but it only needs to be convenient for you and not everyone you're serving. If it's most convenient to use your own garage, then so be it.

Do you wish to connect an artist in Alaska with really cool materials from Florida, but you live in the Midwest? Then an online material exchange might work best for you.

No matter the primary focus of your mission (arts, education, environment, etc.), considering your audience (both donors and shoppers) will help inform what shape, physically and logisti-cally, your creative reuse center will take.

No one type is better than the other – but one is best for your mission.

11 Facing the Inevitable: The Business Plan

In this chapter you will learn:

- The reasons for having a business plan
- The benefits of having a thorough business plan
- Sources for alternative business planning

Now that you've created your mission statement, what type of venue will you need to fulfill your mission?

We're often asked if a business plan is absolutely necessary to get a new creative reuse center off the ground. The unfortunate answer is absolutely yes. It's unfortunate because if your passion is to start a creative reuse center, you're likely to be more tapped into your right brain and taking on a structured business plan may not be your cup of tea. You may feel more comfortable with creative, free-form, intuitive, non-linear thinking. A business plan is about as left brained as a process gets. Think of it as your road map to success. For now, you'll need to put on your analytical, fact-based, sequential hat -- at least for much of the work

So why is it so important to have a business plan – a concept that seems so 1980? Really, the process of creating the plan is almost as critical as the plan itself. You'll think through every aspect of running a business, test your theories and find out if you and your stakeholders are on the same page. Once you have this road map, it will be indispensable. You will have a sound basis for:

- Communicating your idea to stakeholders, funders and fans
- Writing grants
- Seeking fiscal sponsorship
- Recruiting volunteers
- Deciding whether to be mobile, brick and mortar or an online exchange
- Developing partnerships
- Showing credibility with other professionals

There's no absolute right way to create a business plan, but a solid one should have these elements:

Executive Summary

The Executive Summary gives the highlights of your business plan. A potential sponsor, investor or funder will be interested in seeing this summary in an initial proposal. You can use parts of it as a marketing piece or in creating your annual report

Company Overview

The company overview reflects your vision and values. It tells the story of who you are, why you exist, and what difference you make in the community.

Competitive Analysis

This is the "what's up?" with the reuse community in your region. It can also focus on the crafting/DIY market, art supply stores, sustainability education, and other areas where there are people doing what you do. Well, no one is doing exactly what you do. But your audience may be thinking about someone else (Michael's, for instance) when they are on the hunt for crafting supplies.

Marketing Plan

This is how you'll get the audience to think about your creative reuse center first (instead of Michael's) when they want creative supplies. This is where you communicate your uniqueness and goodness in the community.

Financial Plan

Your financial plan will include an operating budget and what plans you have in place to fund the budget. Sales projections could also be included here in this section.

Management and Personnel Plan

So, who's going to do what? That's an important area to think through and document. At the onset, your primary workers are likely to be volunteers. While volunteers will always continue to provide valuable support to your organization, they are most critical at the time that you are raising operating funds and creating your vision.

Action Plan

This is how you'll get from having a great idea to opening your doors. This is fun to brainstorm, but be sure and keep your ultra-practical hat on, too.

Operating Plan

The chapter on infrastructure will be helpful in building a plan for how to keep this baby rolling once you've opened the doors.

We recommend getting a guide for creating a business plan from the library, a friend, or the Internet. There are truckloads of books written by business experts about how to create a compelling business plan. A resource that we love for creative folk like you is *The Right-Brain Business Plan* by Jennifer Lee. It is designed to engage in a creative process to produce your business plan. Her website, rightbrainbusinessplan.com, offers tutorials, webinars, and loads of support in creating a business plan masterpiece.

The process can be fun, imaginative, exciting, and stimulating. But, alas, there is the challenge of putting your ideas and solid planning into a form and language that communicates old school. You will need to straddle the fence that separates pure creative ingenuity from brass tacks facts and figures. You'll get it done and have some fun in the process.

Operative phrase to remember: You'll get it done.

12 Stakeholders: It Takes a Village to Support a Community-Based Organization

In this chapter you will learn:

- That there are many types of individuals invested in your success
- That different stakeholders have different needs
- That it's helpful to vary your communication styles and methods with different groups of stakeholders

Your creative reuse center exists within a community. You already know that having strong relationships with your community members is invaluable. The staff, volunteers, neighbors, sister reuse organizations, funders, participants in your programs, users of your services, retail shoppers, early adopters, environmental fans, arts fans, educators, and government officials all make up your village. They are otherwise known as stakeholders. They all have a stake in what you do because they help facilitate your development, are affected by your activities, and/or share passion for the mission.

You'll want to sit down with your advisory board and have a good brainstorming session about your stakeholder village. In the first activity of this chapter, you can list each stakeholder group, their needs and expectations, and then prioritize them by how important they are to the success of your mission. Once you've gotten clear on who your stakeholders are, it's time to get reflective about your stakeholder relationships.

How well do you know and understand your stakeholders? Do you know how they feel about your project? What do they want to know from you? Do they think you're on the right track? Often those close to your project don't feel comfortable weighing in about your creative reuse center unless they are asked. So, ask! Their feedback will be valuable in creating perspective about where you are and where you are going.

Finally, how do you find out what they think? One of the best ways to get information is to ask them directly. This can be informal and personal. Sitting down and discussing your organization with a donor or volunteer can reveal interesting insights. It can also be formalized in a well-constructed survey. However you approach it, the information is critical to receive and understand.

We are big fans of surveys. We find that the more data collected and analyzed, the better informed we are about our function in the stakeholder village. Without establishing feedback loops, you could be preaching to the choir, working in a silo, and worse, potentially developing programs and services that please you but don't resonate with your stakeholders. At the end of this chapter, there is a sample volunteer survey from Survey Monkey that you might adapt to get feedback from your stakeholder groups.

It is incumbent upon the leaders of a successful creative reuse center to manage stakeholders well. This means understanding how they wish to interact with you. Here are tips for managing a few of the primary stakeholder groups:

Funders

Funders are interested in hearing about your successes and challenges. They generally want those all-important metrics: how many people you served, whether you met your sales and programming goals, how much growth you experienced during the funding period. They want to know how well you managed your resources, if you did what you said you would do, and whether you did it efficiently. They also want to know if you needed to course-correct along the way. They likely appreciate transparency about the areas of the funded project that are not going as planned. Don't wait until the year-end report to communicate with them. Bring them in on the challenges. Often they have sound advice and can help problem-solve the unexpected snags.

Volunteers

Your volunteers are a valuable source of feedback. They are not only contributing to your success, they are in a key position to observe interactions with customers and other stakeholders. Volunteers are generally pleased to be asked their thoughts and opinions about the organization. They also want to be kept in the loop on the organization. Some nonprofits refer to their volunteers as "unpaid staff." If you take that perspective, it is important to inform them of job openings, new employees, new programs, opportunities, events, and organizational changes. Sending to them annual or semi-annual surveys soliciting their feedback is helpful to you and lets them know how valuable their views are to you.

Customers

Your customers expect to have a positive experience at your creative reuse center. They are the experts on how positive that experience is. Getting feedback from them can be very helpful. They will appreciate the opportunity to share with you, especially if they are big fans. If they sign up for your newsletter, they expect that you will reach out to them on a regular, but not too frequent, basis. They will expect to be apprised of changes in policies that affect accessibility. They will be pleased to hear about special events and opportunities. Sending annual or semi-annual surveys to customers on your email list can provide a wealth of (sometimes very surprising) information. And, they will be pleased that you reached out to them.

Google and Survey Monkey are two free survey applications that are easy to use. You can tailor your survey to each stakeholder group. The results are dropped into a spreadsheet or other usable format for your analysis. Some of the online tools have helpful tutorials so you can get the most out of your survey instrument.

Activity: Stakeholders – Name and Rank

Brainstorm with your advisory board a list of specific stakeholders. Include their needs and expectations. Give them a priority rank so that you are clear on where to focus the most time and energy.

We have included a sample to get you started. Your list is likely going to include volunteers, community supporters, donors (material), donors (financial), and government officials.

Stakeholder	Needs and Expectations	Priority
Advisory Board	Updates on progress, monthly financials, notifications of opportunities/ challenges, monthly meetings, consistent interaction with the executive director	1

Sample Volunteer Survey from Survey Monkey

1. In a typical month, about how many hours do you volunteer?

2. How meaningful was the volunteer work you did for this organization?
   - *Extremely meaningful*
   - *Very meaningful*
   - *Moderately meaningful*
   - *Slightly meaningful*
   - *Not at all meaningful*

3. How easy was it to receive the required volunteer training at this organization?
   - *Extremely easy*
   - *Very easy*
   - *Moderately easy*
   - *Slightly easy*
   - *Not at all easy*

4. How useful were the volunteer training sessions at this organization?
   - *Extremely useful*
   - *Very useful*
   - *Moderately useful*
   - *Slightly useful*
   - *Not at all useful*

5. How easy was it to get along with the other volunteers at this organization?
   - *Extremely easy*
   - *Very easy*
   - *Moderately easy*
   - *Slightly easy*
   - *Not at all easy*

6. How easy was it to get along with the staff at this organization?
   - *Extremely easy*
   - *Very easy*
   - *Moderately easy*
   - *Slightly easy*
   - *Not at all easy*

7. How appreciated did your volunteer supervisor make you feel?
   - *Extremely appreciated*
   - *Very appreciated*
   - *Moderately appreciated*
   - *Slightly appreciated*
   - *Not at all appreciated*

8. Overall, were you satisfied with your volunteer experience with this organization, neither satisfied nor dissatisfied with it, or dissatisfied with it?
   - *Extremely satisfied*
   - *Moderately satisfied*
   - *Slightly satisfied*
   - *Neither satisfied nor dissatisfied*
   - *Slightly dissatisfied*
   - *Moderately dissatisfied*
   - *Extremely dissatisfied*

9. How likely are you to continue volunteering at this organization?

- *Extremely likely*
- *Very likely*
- *Moderately likely*
- *Slightly likely*
- *Not at all likely*

10. How likely are you to recommend this organization to others as a place to volunteer?

- *Extremely likely*
- *Very likely*
- *Moderately likely*
- *Slightly likely*
- *Not at all likely*

13 Creating a Buzz: Engaging the Community

In this chapter you will learn:

- About multiple channels for reaching a target audience
- About the value of suiting up and showing up
- To tell your story – it's yours to tell

Creating a buzz means getting people to talk about your project. It means communicating with the community in smart and engaging ways. You'll know you have created buzz when you go to a networking event and nearly everyone has heard of your creative reuse center. They read about it in the local paper. A friend posted on Facebook. They saw your video on YouTube. A friend of a friend said, "You've got to check this out!" They are enticed and intrigued, and you have an audience ready to hear your story.

Remember the days when communication for community causes was almost exclusively mailing campaigns? Periodically organizations would reach out with a hard-to-resist emotional appeal letter meant to break through the clutter and entice your spirit of giving. And phone calls at dinnertime? Like the quarterly appeal phone calls from your alma mater? It's so 20th century.

Nowadays, there are much more interesting, impactful, and creative ways to share your story.

Communication Channels

Social Media

The smart organization engages the audience in a variety of interactive media, including Facebook, Twitter, Pinterest, Google+ and more (seemingly) every day. They use it wisely by posting interesting content, photos, and videos that engages their audience and inspires them to share your message with their friends and fans.

Earned Media

This is another avenue for creating excitement about your creative reuse center. A great example of getting free coverage is SCRAP in Denton, Texas. This North Texas town of 100,000 is a natural fit for a creative reuse center, with strong sustainability initiatives, two major universities, and a vibrant art and craft community. The savvy director contacted the local newspaper, City Council, Chamber of Commerce, and other members of the reuse and arts community. The buzz started from day one. The local newspaper and the newspaper from one of the local universities (with 35,000 students), both ran stories heralding the packed-house grand opening.

Informal Partnerships

Linking up with other community-based organizations is a great way to get your name and mission out while building credibility. When a nonprofit asks for a material donation, ask them to give you credit with your logo on their website or a sign at the event.

Community Events

Be at every community event where you can spread the word, share an interactive activity, and invite the community to share in the fun of building a creative reuse resource.

Civic Groups

Participation in the Chamber of Commerce, City Club, or local business association will give you credibility as a business. And, in a room full of insurance agents, bankers, and florists, you'll inevitably be the coolest kid at the party.

Environmental/Arts/Professional Groups

Joining the local chapter of Reuse Alliance and the Creative Reuse Association will go a long way in showing your commitment to creative reuse and your community. You'll meet the most interesting people who are likely to share your passion. Is there an Etsy or Craftsy group in your town? Green Drinks? If not, start one up!

Rule of Seven

When you first start up, you want to pull out all the buzz-worthy stops. You're working to build a critical mass of information. Remember the Rule of Seven from advertising? Reportedly, people need to hear a message a minimum of seven times before they act on it. If you are using email, newsletters, LinkedIn, Facebook and Twitter, you're priming the pump to pay attention to the buzz.

Suit Up and Show Up

Your message to your audience is the story of your creative reuse center. Chances are there is nothing like it in your community. Personal stories hit home with most people. When a friend or acquaintance hears your compelling tale of stumbling upon a treasure in the incoming donations, it will be hard to hold them back from having their own creative reuse experience. Have that elevator speech down and a fun personal story to share. It's your story to tell. Your excitement and enthusiasm is bound to be contagious.

Get out there! Shake hands, share an interactive project, post a video, wear a piece of repurposed jewelry, and evangelize for creative reuse. There are loads of channels for reaching your audience.

14 All About the Money

In this chapter you will learn:

- About a variety of resources for for-profit ventures
- About a variety of resources for nonprofit ventures

Fundraising, friend raising, crowd, corporate donors, individual donors, loans...all are ways of fund development for your creative reuse center.

There are some distinct areas of difference between doing business as a for-profit and a nonprofit organization. This is one of those areas. You cannot offer a return on investment for an interested donor as a nonprofit, but in most cases, you can offer a tax deduction to friends, fans, and funders.

Whether you are a for-profit or a nonprofit, you are going to need revenue to get off the ground. The methods for raising money vary depending upon your business structure. While many of the principles are the same between finding investors and finding funders, the sources will be different.

If you decide to become a for-profit venture, you have a variety of methods of getting the money together. You can't offer your investors a tax deduction, but you can offer a return on investment or other stake in your company. You may be looking at raising your operating funds from traditional loans, government loans, or investor-based venture capital. There are even arts grants that may be available for a community-based arts program. The Federal Small Business Administration offers loan programs for business start-ups that may not qualify for traditional loans. You should work with your lender to meet the qualifications for an SBA program. There are Microloans, CAPline loans, and many other options to consider.

If you are going in a nonprofit direction, you can research grant funding. You can get valuable information about what grantors are funding for arts or environmental projects in your area. We've found the most versatile funding research tool is the Foundation Center. Many libraries have this resource available to the public.

Few major foundations will be willing to fund operations for an organization without a financial track record. You may wish to focus on small family or investor-advised foundations. That is not to say that writing grants is a bad idea, but we recommend having other irons in the fire. Think outside the box, get creative, and reach out to the community. If community members are excited about your idea, they will invest time or money – or both. If you have wealthy donors, lucky you! If you don't, don't despair. As people become engaged with your idea, they will want to see it happen and prosper. The more people that are invested, even at a modest sum, the better for your success.

Both for-profits and nonprofits may pursue contracts with your local waste management bureau. You may qualify as a materials depot, as you will provide a home for hard to recycle arts materials. Waste hauling companies may be a source of funding, as well.

Crowdfunding (also known as crowdsourcing) has proven successful for a number of big ideas, both for-profit and nonprofit. Generally through the Internet, crowdfunding platforms allow loads of people from loads of places to pitch in for your creative reuse center. You'll want to choose your crowdfunding platform carefully, though. Some have a tipping point. If you don't achieve your stated goal, you don't receive any of the funds committed to your cause. Some allow nonprofits to participate, but not for-profit projects. And vice versa.

An event is one of the most effective ways to raise start-up funds and engage the community in your idea. Donated space, food, beverages, silent auction items, and volunteers can be pulled together for a no- to low-cost event that raises money and gives you a forum for demonstrating the unique attributes of your cool creative reuse center. It is especially effective to have barrels of reused creative materials there for sale. You can set up tables where volunteers lead guests in reused make-and-take projects. The possibilities are endless.

An important tip: Diversify your fund development channels.

15 Risky Business

An unfortunate incident

Belinda (not her real name) was a super star volunteer at SCRAP. She showed up regularly for her shifts and worked diligently stocking and organizing store sections. During a typical shift, she was cleaning up the wood section, which needed badly to be organized. As she was moving varying sizes of wood, a piece with a sharp point fell, penetrated her thin, plastic shoe, and went right through her big toe. Apparently this piece of wood was balanced precariously between two other larger pieces. As they were moved, the sharp piece dropped to the ground. Belinda was new to town, worked as a nanny part-time, and did not have medical insurance.

This unfortunate incident was indeed a wake-up call for us that mitigating risk does not just mean having contracts, liability insurance, and criminal background checks in place. It also means ensuring the physical safety and well being for staff and volunteers.

What we did right:
- We had First Aid-trained staff and a well-stocked First Aid kit.
- We had an incident report template.
- We had a closed-toe shoe policy.

What we did not do right:
- We did not have insurance that covered injury to volunteers (in many states volunteers are covered by Worker's Compensation—but not our state).
- We did not have a written protocol for how to handle an emergency.
- We did not have safety standards in place that would have prevented the wood from being stacked precariously.
- We did not have a sturdy closed-toe shoe policy.

Actions Taken:
- We have an insurance policy that covers medical costs for volunteer injuries.
- We assembled a safety committee, and created a safety manual with protocols to manage situations ranging from robberies to stacking boxes properly.

There are numerous areas of risk to consider for your creative reuse center. As this isn't meant to be a comprehensive risk management manual, we offer resources to do further research at the back of the book.

Space Safety Management
Every organization should have safety policies that are easy to access. It is equally important as to have safety policies in place and ensure all of your workers and volunteers are oriented and familiar with them. At a minimum, be sure you have a First Aid kit, CPR-trained person onsite, and a fire extinguisher from the moment you open your doors.

This is a general policy provided by Health and Safety Executive (hse.gov.uk):

Statement of general policy

To prevent accidents and cases of work-related ill health and provide adequate control of health and safety risks arising from work activities

To provide adequate training to ensure employees are competent to do their work

To engage and consult with employees on day-to-day health and safety conditions and provide advice and supervision on occupational health

To implement emergency procedures - evacuation in case of fire or other significant incident. You can find help with your fire risk assessment at: _____

To maintain safe and healthy working conditions, provide and maintain plant, equipment and machinery, and ensure safe storage / use of substances

Health and safety law poster is displayed:

First-aid box and accident book are located:

Accidents and ill health at work reported under RIDDOR: (Reporting of Injuries, Diseases and Dangerous Occurrences Regulations)

Receiving Material Donations
There are numerous potential hazards involved with taking in and sorting donations from unknown sources. A few include:

- Heavy boxes
- Sharp objects
- Hazardous compounds
- Broken glass
- Syringes
- Insects and vectors
- Mold
- Wet or unstable containers

You should have policies and protective gear to ensure safety for those who are receiving, sorting, and moving material donations.

Professional Relationships

Legal

You will need an attorney whether you are for-profit or nonprofit. There are aspects of business that must be handled by legal experts. They include:

- Contracted relationships
- Human resource policies and issues
- Compliance with federal and state laws and statutes
- Waivers
- 501(c)(3) compliance (for nonprofits)
- Assessment of risk

Financial

A CPA and bookkeeper are important professionals to engage in your creative reuse center from day one. A bookkeeper can set up your chart of accounts, reconcile your bank statements, prepare your monthly profit and loss reports, and help you keep an eye on the day-to-day money flow. A bookkeeper need not be a staff position. There are highly qualified freelance bookkeepers that have specialty areas, such as nonprofit accounting.

Working with your bookkeeper, your CPA will file taxes on your behalf. If you are a nonprofit that will be applying for large foundation grants, you may be required to have annual financial audits by a qualified CPA firm.

Your banker will be a valuable resource. In addition to providing a place to keep your hard-earned cash, many banks will provide additional services to small businesses. Bank representatives are a wealth (pun intended) of financial advice. They can also connect you with other business services in the community.

Insurance

There are several insurance needs for a small business of any kind. You will need general liability to protect you and your business from lawsuits stemming from perceived negligence, as well as loss or damage to your physical space. If you have a company vehicle, that will require separate auto insurance. Nonprofits have directors' and officers' insurance to protect individual board members from lawsuits against the organization. Worker's compensation, volunteer injury, and liquor liability insurance are also available.

Mitigating Risk

There are many ways to protect your organization. Anticipating risks and preparing for them is the best way to avoid a nasty legal or financial situation. On the next page is a checklist that covers many areas of risk management.

CHECKLIST: THINGS YOU CAN DO TO MINIMIZE BUSINESS RISKS AND LOSSES

From smallbusiness.findlaw.com

Purchasing business insurance is only one part of minimizing business losses. An effective risk management and loss prevention program will, in most instances, lower your insurance premiums and diminish the probability of filing claims, replacing damaged property, and defending yourself in a lawsuit. Do you:

- Keep your wiring, carpets, stairs, floors, elevators, and escalators in good repair?
- Have a system in place to remove slipping hazards from the floors and stairs?
- Install fire and burglar alarms?
- Isolate flammable materials and products?
- Install high quality locks?
- Keep valuables in a safe?
- Install and maintain lighting that discourages theft?
- Use a security service?
- Let only employees with good driving records drive for you?
- Provide drivers' training?
- Provide ongoing training to minimize injuries from operating machinery?
- Prohibit employees from disabling safety devices on machinery?
- Provide employees with protective gear?
- Teach employees how to lift properly?

- Have, and use, a self-inspection checklist from OSHA to help you identify and minimize employee risk from particular hazards?

- Make sure that your employees' workstations are ergonomically appropriate and that they follow guidelines to avoid injury?

- Keep minimal amounts of cash in your office and in cash registers?

- Keep adequate and updated records of your inventory, accounts receivable, and equipment purchases?

16 Solid Gold: Your Volunteer Team

In this chapter you will learn:

- About recruiting volunteers
- About applications and screening
- The importance of retaining valuable volunteers

Solid gold. That's what volunteers are to an organization. Volunteers can play a variety of roles at your creative reuse center. Depending upon your needs and the volunteers' skill sets and interests, you can have many of your essential functions covered. Volunteers make it possible to accomplish your mission with little or no initial funding. And, when you're ready to hire, you'll have a pool of super stars to choose from that already know the organization, are committed to the mission, and are known to you.

Both of us started out at SCRAP as volunteers. Kelley was the volunteer Volunteer Coordinator and did a year of AmeriCorps service there. Through her volunteer service, she was in a perfect position to be schooled—about creative reuse, nonprofit work, volunteer management, and the organization. Alyssa began her relationship with SCRAP as a store volunteer. Because she became a super star volunteer, she stood out and was clearly a great fit for the organization, she was a prime choice as store manager when that position came available.

Unless you have initial seed money, you will also be starting out your creative reuse career as a volunteer. You will attract other volunteers with your passion, enthusiasm, and love. It's hard work, but there are willing souls out there who want to give back to the community through service. You are doing them a favor by providing the opportunity.

Finding volunteers
First things first: Before you start recruiting, put together volunteer job descriptions. You want to communicate clearly what your needs and expectations are at the onset. Identify the areas where you most need volunteers and fill those slots first. Your advisory board, your first volunteers, are already in place. Now you need heavy lifters to do the work. You need to receive donations, sort and price, stock shelves, ring up sales, table community events, and set up your website. These are all jobs that volunteers can fill.

According to the Corporation for National and Community Service, 25.5% of the population engages in volunteer work. College students, baby boomers, and veterans volunteer at a higher rate. If you happen to live in Utah, you'll never have a shortage of unpaid help. 44.5% of Utah's population volunteers.

Recruiting volunteers means getting the word out about your volunteer needs in many of the same ways you get the word out when you are creating a buzz. Using similar channels, you will want to advertise for volunteers with social media. Your fans and followers will get the message that you are not only open for business, but an excellent place to spend time doing good. You can reach out to prospective volunteers through specific websites and listservs that target your kind of people; creative, sustainability-minded, crafty, engaged in the community, and excited about your mission. Universities, retirement communities, service groups, and corporations are great places to advertise your volunteer needs.

Screening volunteers

Not every person who wants to be a volunteer for your organization should be. A volunteer who is not a good fit will require more of your time and energy in supervision than you can spare. Adopt a volunteer application and screening process to be sure you are choosing the right people for the right tasks. It's hard to decline the services of a willing individual when you have so much work to do. We still advocate that you screen carefully and engage those who are a good fit. You might think of it this way—if you accept the services of those who aren't quite right for the job, you are precluding them from finding volunteer opportunities that are a better fit for their strengths and interests.

Screening volunteers also can mean making sure they are safe and appropriate for the tasks at hand. Physically challenged volunteers should be given tasks appropriate to their abilities. Volunteers working with children should be cleared with a criminal background check before leading a group. Volunteers with dust allergies can be given administrative tasks away from the inevitably dusty store or storage rooms.

We've included a sample volunteer application at the end of this chapter, and you can download a copy from our website.

Retaining volunteers
Finally, once you have your corps of volunteers, treat them like exactly what they are—solid gold. In a recent survey we conducted of volunteers at our creative reuse center, we discovered that volunteers feel valued when they are recognized and given direct feedback. Calling them out, thanking them, offering material discounts, and bringing treats are all great ways of letting them know how valuable they are. Another way to keep volunteers coming back is to match up their interests with tasks the organization needs to have done. Some volunteers are going to have a great sense of satisfaction sweeping the floor and sorting through donations. Other volunteers will be excited to represent you at community events. Still others may lead field trips.

Many organizations consider their volunteers to be "unpaid staff." They are included in decision-making and given annual reviews. These practices also lead to a sense of value and satisfaction for many volunteers.

Volunteer Application

Please complete this application form if you are interested in becoming a SCRAP volunteer.

Contact Information

Name (legal): _____

Nickname? _____

Street: _____

City:_____   State: ____ Zip:_____

Phone: (cell) _____

           (home) _____

           (work) _____

e-mail: _____

Date of Birth: _____/_____/_____

Employer: _____

Employer Phone: _____

E-mail Preferences

We like to keep volunteers informed of important news, schedules and volunteer opportunities by e-mail, however we will not send you any e-mail you prefer not to receive. Use the checkboxes to select the kinds of e-mail you would like to receive from us.

☐ SCRAP newsletter (one to two times monthly)

☐ Volunteer newsletter (monthly)

How did you hear about us?

Why would you like to volunteer at SCRAP?

Interests & Hobbies:
What interests you? What do you like to do?

Skills:
Please mark those that apply to you:

☐ Organizing ☐ Administrative Skills
☐ Child Education ☐ Events
☐ Community Engagement
☐ Managing People ☐ OLCC License ☐ Cashiering
☐ Other _____

Is there anything else we should know about your availability or skills?

What is Your Availability?

☐ Weekly 3 hour shift in retail store
☐ On-going non-retail support ☐ Event support
☐ Other: _____

	M	T	W	Th	F	S	Su
10am-1pm	☐	☐	☐	☐	☐	☐	☐
12pm-3pm	☐	☐	☐	☐	☐	☐	☐
3pm-6pm	☐	☐	☐	☐	☐	☐	☐
Evenings	☐	☐	☐	☐	☐	☐	☐

Emergency and Medical Information
This information is confidential and will be used only in the event you require assistance. It will not act as a condition of your acceptance into the volunteer program. In the case of injury, SCRAP has limited liability insurance that covers volunteers.

Emergency Contact

First and Last Name: _____

Relationship: _____

Phone: (cell)_____

             (home) _____

             (work) _____

Do you require any special accommodations in your work area? If so, please describe. ☐ Yes   ☐ No

Do you have emergency medical conditions or allergies of which we or emergency personnel should be aware? If so, please describe.   ☐ Yes   ☐ No

Please read the following before you sign.

Permission to Use Material and Photos: I agree to allow SCRAP to take photographs of me and/or my creative work at SCRAP events or at SCRAP. I agree to allow SCRAP to images of me or my work for SCRAP promotions or other legitimate purposes.
☐ Yes   ☐ No

Volunteer Release Statement: As a condition of my participation with SCRAP, I hereby release SCRAP and its agents, associates and related parties from all responsibility for personal injuries to me and damages to my property sustained in the performance of my volunteer activities.

1. Nondiscrimination Statement: It is the policy of SCRAP to maintain an environment free of discrimination, including harassment. SCRAP prohibits discrimination and harassment against any person because of age, ancestry, color, disability or handicap, national origin, race, religious creed, sex, sexual orientation or veteran status.

2.Background Checks: There are some volunteer positions at SCRAP where a Criminal Background Check may be required. I understand that if I refuse to release records, I may not be able to fulfill these positions.

I have read and understand the above. If needed, I have asked questions of the Volunteer Coordinator to clarify these statements to my satisfaction. I agree.

Volunteer Signature _____

Date _____

Legal Guardian (if applicant has legal guardian)

_____

Date _____

17 Infrastructure

In this chapter you will learn:
- A strong infrastructure offers a strong foundation for your organization
- To stick to the basics
- Investing in building the infrastructure will allow you to focus on the mission

The enemy of infrastructure is chaos – and you should avoid it at all costs. By virtue of the fact that you're dealing with donated materials, setting up a creative reuse center is already unpredictable enough. Having systems in place will save your sanity when you're up to your ears in fabric, bottle tops, paper, and crayons.

While there are many elements to building capacity in your creative reuse center, we'll stick to the basics. There are so many self-help business books, electronic devices and programs, online seminars, and forums that it's easy to get distracted and overwhelmed. While starting out, we recommend that you, too, stick to the basics.

- Decision-making
- Staff/Volunteers

- Programs
- Administration
- Communication

Decision-making

From the outset, plan who is responsible for what decisions and how they will be made. In a nonprofit, you have a board of directors who has legal and financial responsibility for the organization. With that duty, the board has the obligation to be the ultimate decision maker on governance, legal, financial and, sometimes, operational matters. You and your designees will manage the daily nuts and bolts decisions. You'll determine how much decision-making power to give your lead volunteers. You may equip them to be leaders you can rely on to train and supervise other volunteers.

There are as many styles of decision-making as there are personalities. Some people are quick and decisive. Others take considerable time in reviewing all the possibilities and potential pitfalls. And there is every style in between these two.

Management experts generally define the process of decision-making with some version of these steps:

1. Defining the problem
2. Identifying potential obstacles
3. Developing possible alternatives
4. Analyzing those alternatives
5. Selecting the best option
6. Implementing the decision
7. Evaluating the outcome

Make a plan of how decisions will be made, document it and consistently implement the plan. When employees and volunteers can rely on a pattern of decision-making, it creates a strong, safe, collaborative environment.

Staff/Volunteers

In a start-up, the major players (maybe including you) are volunteers. Your trusted volunteers become critical to creating the infrastructure. Someone has to be available to take donations, sell materials, communicate your message in the community, and take care of business. These trusted volunteers serve critical roles in establishing your creative reuse center.

Job descriptions are helpful in making the implementation of your mission run smoothly. That can be a challenge in a place where there is more work to be done than people to do it. It is an advantage to present a model of flexibility and fluidity. You can firm up role distinctions as your creative reuse center grows, becomes financially viable, and you start to build a staff.

Programs
Your programs will likely begin with retail, reuse and recovery (donations), and community outreach. Setting up programs includes setting goals, plans of action for implementation, ways to measure your progress, and ways to pay for it. One of the beauties of a creative reuse center is that you have a built-in moneymaker in selling the donated materials you are recovering from the waste stream.

As we discussed in the first chapter of this book, a creative reuse center develops organically based on the visionaries behind the project. If the leader is a former schoolteacher, having an education program may rise to the top of the list of programs once the store is established. If the leader is an artist or crafter, a boutique, gallery, or studio space may be a higher priority. But all creative reuse centers and budding new organizations need to do community outreach. If you aren't showing up on the community calendar and events, it will be difficult to demonstrate the creative reuse concept to the community.

Administration
You may not need all of these systems at the start of your development, but plan to have platforms in place that will allow you to accommodate growth. Because you're taking care of business and consulting this book, you will be facing growth.

Reliable computer and monitor
There are electronic recyclers in many communities. They sometimes sell or donate computer equipment to community-

based organizations. A resource for nonprofits called TechSoup offers donations of hardware and software for a licensing fee.

Accounting system
Systems that are electronic and cloud-based are most handy for start-ups. If your accounting system is accessible from any computer in any location, you and your bookkeeper can take care of business at home, in a coffee shop, or onsite.

Database
You've got to start, from the beginning, keeping track of donors, volunteers, and valued customers. There are hundreds of client relationship management systems or even spreadsheet-based programs. The important thing is to document activities and keep the database updated at all times.

Communications

Bulk communications program
Your newsletters can be personalized and sent out in bulk without fear of spamming with excellent communication systems like Constant Contact, Emma, and Vertical Response. Always ask for a nonprofit or start-up rate. Many of these vendors will offer free use up to a certain number of communications per month.

Website
We live in a world where we no longer have to hire a web developer, designer, and coder to have a website. With WordPress, Noodle, or other easy-to-use format, you can create your own site. You can purchase a URL and get web hosting quickly and easily. Down the road when you are established, you'll no doubt want a fancier shmancier web presence but for now, get yourself on the Internet so others can find you.

Social Media
Social media is the primary means for many of our target audience to get information. If social media is used in an interesting and informative way, the effects can be synergistic. When new information is shared from a trusted source (a friend or a "friend"

or from someone a "friend" knows), it is all the more interesting and powerful. You can help create buzz, promote events, share the message of creative reuse, and interact with new audiences. Get on board with Twitter and Facebook if you aren't already!

Get this infrastructure in place at the start and you'll be in excellent shape to focus your valuable time and energy on getting the creative reuse center off the ground.

18 Setting Up Your Creative Reuse Center

In this chapter you will learn:

- How day-to-day at your creative reuse center can be unpredictable
- The difference between a traditional retail environment and a creative reuse center
- How to physically set up your retail space
- How to determine your sorting process
- How to create a pricing structure

A creative reuse center can be a magical, creative haven—a place where one can wander, dig, and see what the mind imagines. It can also be a place of chaos and unpredictability. Part of the je ne sais quoi of reuse is that it's hard to imagine the types of materials (and types of people, for that matter!) that will come your way.

While the creative reuse center might include other features like a gallery, boutique, library, or workshop space, the biggest chunk of square footage (and the bread and butter!) of most creative reuse centers is the retail store. If you've ever worked in a retail environment, that experience is, of course, very valuable in training your customer service and money handling skills, but that's about it.

Imagine, if you will, walking into your nearest big box store to buy laundry detergent. First of all, you probably know right where it will be, in the aisle marked with "Laundry" or "Cleaning Supplies." You arrive in the aisle to find 20 different choices—powder or liquid, this brand or that, spring fresh or lavender, stain fighting or color saving, etc. So, you choose exactly what you need and likely walk away a satisfied customer.

A typical retail approach doesn't apply in the world of creative reuse. In a creative reuse center, you can't just order more of Product A from the manufacturer when you run out. You will hope that more of Product A or a close substitute will be donated to you. A customer may be looking for something specific that you don't have, but (not to be defeated) you help them come up with a creative solution using the materials that you do have available. First you could check the "Plastics" section, or maybe something in the "Wood" section might work? You have the opportunity in this situation to alter that person's perception and relationship to materials. Sure, a wheel is a wheel, but couldn't a plastic bottle cap or half of a metal spool be a wheel, too?

While not nearly as easy to organize as a grocery store, or even a big box craft store, you'll want your store to be as shop-able and navigable as possible. Adding some structure and policies to these basic categories is essential:

- Receiving Material Donations
- Flow
- Sorting and Packaging
- Pricing
- Sections
- Signage
- Payment for Goods and Services

Receiving Material Donations

Make a list of the materials you will take and those items you cannot accept. That list should be made easily accessible to the public on your website and with signage at your location.

You will need a consistent protocol for every donation that comes through the door:

1. Examine boxes and bags of donations carefully. Only take desirable items that are clean, usable and fit your materials criteria.

2. Weigh the items you receive and note them on a daily log sheet.

3. Return the materials to the donor that you are unable to take with a smile and a recommendation for alternatives for those materials. It is helpful to have a resource list to give your donors with other reuse organizations that may be able to receive the donated items you cannot take.

4. If it is a tax deductible donation, offer the donor a receipt that includes:

   • The date

   • Weight of materials received as donation

   • Tax deductible ID number

Flow

In trail building and repair, it is helpful to run down the trail imagining that you are water to see where the water may bank, or pool, or erode the ground. You can then plan accordingly where you should put in rocks, waterbars, and other features to prevent future problems. Thusly, when setting up your retail space, you will want to imagine the flow of materials, from donation (intake) to display to sales. Efficient flow of materials could include:

• A well-marked area for donation intake, connected to, but somehow separated from the store, such as a garage or walled-off corner.

• Adequate (temporary!) storage space for donations awaiting processing. The quicker you can process the donations, the better, but the reality is that materials may pile up before your very eyes. Too many donations is a good challenge to have, but a challenge nonetheless.

- Space for sorting and processing donations. One system that works well is to have bins on shelves that coordinate to sections of the store. That way, you can sort a super miscellaneous box easily into more specific sections. Then, take that bin out to the appropriate section without extraneous handling of materials.
- Store fixtures that comfortably display the various materials. This could be shelves with clear bins, barrels on the floor, and/or specific fixtures such as greeting card or magazine displays.
- Shopping baskets, boxes, or carts for shoppers to collects their purchases.

Sorting and Packaging

Not only will you need to have the space for sorting and packaging, but you'll need to decide how you want to sort and package your materials. That is, will you individually package and price most items, or will you put out big bins for patrons to dig through, or some other combination?

Some materials sell better packaged. Take colorful ribbons that are off the spool. They may sell better packaged up in packs with complimentary colors and types than in a basket to sell singly. If you plan to package materials, you'll want to collect the packaging and consider whether or not you'll have a steady supply of that type, shape, and size of container. Other materials are best sold in bulk. Wine corks, colorful bottle tops, architectural design samples, pens, crayons and binder strips can be sold by the scoop, handful or bagful.

Pricing

Pricing directly influences sorting and packaging, and vice versa. It's helpful to establish a rule of thumb, such as your prices are approximately 25% of the average retail price. This guideline is a good place to start for your straightforward materials like fabric, office supplies, notions, paint or cardstock.

You'll receive more unique materials such as one-time manufacturers' over runs or printer's errors. To find an appropriate price point, you will want to consider customer demand, the coolness factor and creative potential. You may research a particularly unique or potentially valuable item to find the retail value before determining how to price it.

Sections
How will you categorize your materials? By physical make-up (plastic, metal, paper, etc.)? By use (collage, sewing, printmaking, etc.)? By color? Alphabetized? We wouldn't recommend the last one, but the point is, you can set up whatever system of categories works for your center. Just be sure to keep it consistent and well-labeled, so your customers will know where to possible look for an obscure item.

Signage
In a creative reuse center, you are dealing with sensory overload. Signage is essential to help customers make sense of your space and your inventory.

Consider clearly marking sections to create structure and organization. Section signs can identify materials; wood, metal, fabric, plastic, ceramic. Or, they can designate types of products; office supplies, collage, craft, notions, architectural design.

Signage for merchandise should clearly display the name of the item, the price, and the unit (per pound, per inch, per bag). Just for fun, creative reuse lends itself to signage might include descriptive adjectives, puns, or suggestions of uses for the materials.

Payment for Goods and Services
There are many ways to accept payment for your products, workshops, fieldtrips and donations. You may be sufficiently high tech to do all of your business electronically with your iPad, a point-of-sale system and electronic cash box. Or, you may choose a cash-only system with a locking cash box.

You need a cash tracking system to be used without fail. Using a daily sales sheet, your basic procedure will include:

- Count the till at the start of the day (event)
- Count the cash, checks and credit card purchases at the close of the day
- Fill out the daily sales sheet in full, noting discrepancies

- Count out the till for the next day (event)
- Fill out a bank deposit slip for the cash/checks and place in an envelope sealed and marked with the date. Initial the envelope across the seal
- Either place in a safe onsite or make daily bank deposits

Cash

A cash register is relatively inexpensive. You can purchase one from Office Depot for less than $150. Of course used is more desirable, less expensive but more risky. You definitely want a reliable way of taking, changing and securing cash.

Debit/Credit cards

Even the smallest operation can now take credit cards using a Square or other device to take credit cards directly on their smart phone. There is a percentage fee, but it expands your options for taking payment. Many people no longer carry cash and depend upon the ability to use a credit or debit card for purchases.

Checks

In an era of electronic purchasing, writing checks is reserved for paying the rent and bills that can't be paid with a bill-pay system through the bank. There will be the occasional old-school customer who wants to write a check. If you determine you will receive checks as payment, it is wise to check ID carefully and ask for a phone number.

These are a few basic tips to start you off. You will set up your creative reuse center to maximize your space, fit your personality, meet the demands of your customers and keep incoming donations and outgoing sales flowing. You will show off your creative flair and love for the mission in your own way.

There are many things that will come up for you along the way:

- Branding
- Web presence
- Job descriptions for creative reuse
- Associations and other support

Final Word

The creative reuse movement has been around for nearly 40 years. In the last decade, it seems to have exploded all over the country. You are on the cutting edge of an exciting movement in reuse history.

Starting a creative reuse center takes a certain type of social entrepreneur that can not only remain calm and think clearly in chaotic situations, but also make snap decisions based on gut feeling and experience. It takes someone who can manage the unpredictability inherent in this kind of project. There will be hours with very few customers, only a couple of donations, and no workshops or field trips scheduled. And then – bam! – you will turn around and there is a huge line of customers, a large truck just pulled up with 4 pallets of donations, and all of your volunteers have called out.

Never fear! You can manage it. Right?

Our hope is that you have decided that you are exactly the type of person with that kind of passion to start up a creative reuse center. We further hope that this manual will be a helpful and ready resource as you move forward. We wish you the greatest joy and sense of accomplishment in helping the community, helping the planet and creating economic opportunities.

We invite you to contribute to our blog at

www.creativereuseworkshop.org

Post photos! Ask questions! Share ideas!

Yours in creative reuse forever,

Kelley and Alyssa

Additional Resources

For more information about topics in this book, below is a list of some of our favorite sites, books and articles that you may enjoy.

General

Reuse Alliance

www.reusealliance.org

Creative Reuse Workshop

www.creativereuseworkshop.org

The Anatomy of a Creative Reuse Center

CALIFORNIA

Humboldt

SCRAP Humboldt
www.scraphumboldt.org

Long Beach

Long Beach Depot for Creative Reuse
www.thelongbeachdepot.org

Oakland

East Bay Depot for Creative Reuse
www.creativereuse.org

San Francisco

SCRAP (Scroungers' Center for Reusable Art Parts)
www.scrap-sf.org

Santa Barbara

Art for Scrap
www.artfromscrap.org

CONNECTICUT

Hartford

Scrap-It
www.scrap-it.net

DISTRICT OF COLUMBIA

SCRAP DC
www.scrapdc.org

GEORGIA

Atlanta

WonderRoot Creative Reuse
www.wonderroot.org

Carrollton

The Scrap Bin
www.scrapbin.org

ILLINOIS

Chicago

Creative Reuse Warehouse
www.resourcecenterchicago.org

MASSACHUSETTS

Cambridge
Extras for Creative Learning (EXCL)
www.exclrecycles.org

MICHIGAN

Ann Arbor
The Scrap Box
www.scrapbox.org

Detroit
Arts and Scraps
www.artsandscraps.org

Traverse City
SCRAP TC
www.scraptc.org

NORTH CAROLINA

Asheville
Trash, Inc.
www.trashincasheville.com

Cary
Cary Creative Center
www.carycreativecenter.org

Durham
The Scrap Exchange
www.scrapexchange.org

Hickory
Resource Warehouse and Gallery
www.resourcewarehouse.org

NEW YORK

Queens, Long Island City
Materials for the Arts
www.mfta.org

OHIO

Toledo
Scrap4Art
www.scrap4arttoledo.org

OREGON

Eugene
MECCA
www.materials-exchange.org

Portland
SCRAP (School and Community Reuse Action Project)
www.scrappdx.org

PENNSYLVANIA

Lancaster
Lancaster Creative Reuse
www.lancastercreativereuse.org

Pittsburgh
Pittsburgh Center for Creative Reuse
www.pccr.org

TEXAS

Austin
Austin Creative Reuse
www.austincreativereuse.org

Denton
SCRAP Denton
www.scrapdenton.org

Houston
Texas Art Asylum
www.texasartasylum.com

Passion and Motivation: What Floats Your Boat?
www.mindtools.com

Self Motivation for the Self Employed: Keep Your Passion Alive and Achieve Your Goals by Martin Edic

www.suite101.com/article/inventory-the-personal-asset-of-passions

Nonprofit? For Profit? Hybrid?
www.charitynetusa.com

www.snpo.org

www.councilofnonprofits.org

www.boardsource.org

www.irs.gov

www.sba.gov

www.entrepreneur.com

A Mother Ship May be in Order: Fiscal Sponsorship
Fiscal Sponsorship – 6 Ways To Do It Right by Gregory L. Colvin

www.tides.org

www.fracturedatlas.org

www.tides.org/community/networks-partners/nnfs/

Feasibility: Is the Community Glue Gun-Ready?
www.readyplanning.com

www.enterprisingnonprofits.ca

www.projectsmart.co.uk

Building Your Advisory Board
The New Effective Voluntary Board of Directors: What It Is and Why It Works by William R. Conrad Jr.

www.nonprofitlawblog.org

www.bridgestar.org

www.boardnetusa.net

Creating your Mission Statement

www.mindtools.com

www.inc.com

www.entrepreneur.com

www.councilofnonprofits.org

www.boardsource.org

Facing the Inevitable: The Business Plan

The Right Brain Business Plan by Jennifer Lee

www.mindtools.com

www.inc.com

www.entrepreneur.com

www.councilofnonprofits.org

www.boardsource.org

Stakeholders: It Takes a Village to Support a Community-Based Organization

www.mindtools.com

www.surveymonkey.com

www.stakeholdermanagement.com

Artful Leadership: Managing Stakeholder Problems in Nonprofit Arts Organizations (Indiana University Center on Philanthropy Series in Governance) by Mary Tschirhart

Creating a Buzz: Engaging the Community

Pinterest for Business: How to Pin Your Company to the Top of the Hottest Social Media Network (Que Biz-Tech) by Jess Loren

The Dragonfly Effect (Quick, Effective and Powerful Ways to Use Social Media to Drive Social Change) by Jennifer Aaker and Andy Smith

Guide to Marketing the Arts in Your Non-Profit Organization - www.nyfa.org/files_uploaded/NYFAMarketingGuide.pdf

All About the Money

Fundraising for Social Change by Kim Klein

The Social Entrepreneur's Handbook: How to Start, Build, and Run a Business That Improves the World by Rupert Scofield

How to Find Business Information: A Guide for Business People, Investors, and Researchers by Lucy Heckman

www.money.cnn.com

Risky Business

www.osha.gov

www.sba.gov

smallbusiness.findlaw.com

Solid Gold: Your Volunteer Team

www.idealist.org

Volunteer Management Handbook (95 Edition) by Tracy Daniel Conners (ed.)

Infrastructure

Not-For-Profit Accounting Made Easy by Warren Ruppel

QuickBooks 2012 the Official Guide by Leslie Capachietti

The Dragonfly Effect (Quick, Effective and Powerful Ways to Use Social Media to Drive Social Change) by Jennifer Aaker and Andy Smith

Acknowledgements

The idea for this manual came about two years ago when we started a fiscal sponsorship for creative reuse centers at SCRAP in Portland, Oregon. Requests for advice started flooding in from all over the country. It became clear that creative reuse was sweeping the nation. We wanted to support all the budding projects. Writing a manual seemed the best way to do it.

I'd like to shout out to those who first influenced me in pursuing a lifestyle of waste reduction and repurposing: Joanna Dyer, Babs Adamski, Stephen Gibbs and Sarah Morgan. These are true advocates of creative reuse in Portland. Along my journey, there have been real champions who have had significant impact on me: Debbie Caselton, Alyssa Kail, Keri Piehl, Lindsey Newkirk, and MaryEllen Etienne.

Thanks to the amazing staff at SCRAP for all they do for creative reuse: Maxwell Bendetti, Timothy Combs, Dryden Driggers, Heather Gregory, Alyssa Kail, Lisa LeDoux, Elizabeth Start, Sanne Stienstra, Stephanie Stoller, and Stephanie Weber. Thanks to the members of the board of directors at SCRAP, who are true creative reuse visionaries: Debbie Caselton, Owen Fritts, Elizabeth Goodman, Karen Shimada, and Kate Stock. Thank you to the bold leaders doing the work from the ground up for SCRAP USA: Heather Bouley, Tibora Girczyc-Blum, Donna Gregory, Karen Klein, and Liz Lancashire.

This project would not have turned out so well without the brilliant and generous help of Jenn Alvin. My deep gratitude to my writing partner, the creative and talented Alyssa Kail. Special thanks to Aaron Duran, Sanne Stienstra and Stephanie Stoller for giving considerable time and talent in editing .

I give all my love and appreciation to my husband, Brian Casey, who makes my life richer and makes me better than I am. Finally, thanks to my mentor and friend, Jon Agee, who inspires me in life and work.

Kelley Carmichael Casey

October 1, 2012

I'd first and foremost like to thank my writing partner, Kelley Carmichael Casey, without whom this project would have never seen the light of day. Thank you for your dedication to expanding reuse globally and your dedication to my professional growth over these many years.

Many thanks to the SCRAPpers of yesterday, today, and tomorrow. I am ever reenergized by the inspiration, innovation, and exuberance creative reuse brings into the world.

A very special thank you to Sanne Stienstra, Aaron Duran, and Stephanie Stoller for crossing our t's, dotting our i's, and your overall editing expertise. And to Jenn Alvin, a true gem, for helping us to pull together, neatly package, and polish this project.

Thank you to my friends, family, and especially my husband for all your love and support.

Alyssa Kail

October 1, 2012

Made in the USA
San Bernardino, CA
20 January 2013